First Facts®

SCIENCE **BASICS**

WHAT IS FORCE?

by Jody S. Rake

Consultant:
Paul Ohmann
Associate Professor
College of Arts and Sciences: Physics
University of St. Thomas

PEBBLE
a capstone imprint

First Facts are published by Pebble,
1710 Roe Crest Drive, North Mankato, Minnesota 56003
www.mycapstone.com

Library of Congress Cataloging-in-Publication Data
Library of Congress Cataloging-in-Publication data is available on the Library of Congress website.
ISBN 978-1-9771-0267-6 (library binding)
ISBN 978-1-9771-0507-3 (paperback)
ISBN 978-1-9771-0273-7 (eBook PDF)

Editorial Credits
Jaclyn Jaycox and Mari Bolte, editors; Kyle Grentz, designer; Eric Gohl, media researcher; Laura Manthe, production specialist

Photo Credits
AP Photo: John Raoux, 19; Capstone Studio: Karon Dubke, 20–21; Shutterstock: Christina Richards, 17, Drazen Vukelic, 9, Prasit Rodphan, 5, saicle, background (throughout), Samot, 15, Todd Taulman Photography, cover, Vasyl Shulga, 7, xtock, 11

Printed in the United States 6216

TABLE OF CONTENTS

LET THE FORCE **MOVE YOU**

Force is a push or a pull. Force happens when two objects come together. When you opened this book, you used force to make the cover move. You use forces every day.

Forces make things move. They can also make a moving object stop. When you kick a ball that is sitting still, it moves. When you catch a moving ball, it stops.

Force can also change the speed and direction of a moving object. The faster you pedal your bike, the faster it moves. If you move the handlebars, the bike changes direction.

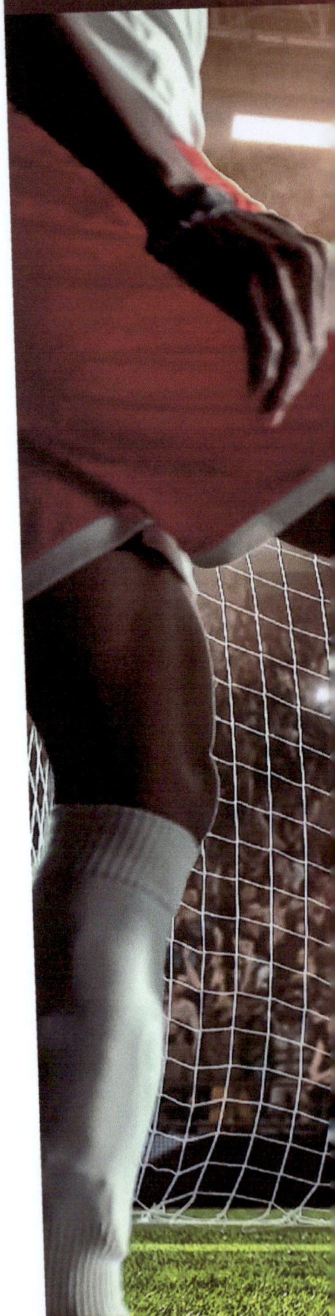

SCIENCE
FRICTION

There are many types of forces. When you roll a toy car across the floor, it will slow down and stop. The force that makes it stop is called ***friction***. Friction happens when one ***surface*** rubs against another. Friction helps you walk. The force of friction on the ground keeps your foot from sliding.

friction—a force made when two objects rub against each other

surface—the outside or outermost area of something

AIR RESISTANCE

Air has its own kind of friction. Air ***resistance*** slows down a moving object. The amount of air resistance depends on the size of the surface. A bigger surface will have more air resistance. This is why a large parachute floats gently to the ground. Something smaller and with less air resistance, such as a rock, will fall faster.

FACT

Some surfaces have more friction than others. A toy car will roll farther on a wood floor than it will on carpet. This is because rough carpet has more friction than smooth wood.

resistance—a force that opposes or slows the motion of an object

A HEAVY SITUATION

Gravity is a force that pulls two objects together. Earth has gravity. Without gravity, the spinning Earth would fling us off the planet and into space. Gravity gives things weight. Bigger objects usually have more weight because of gravity.

FACT

The weight of an object can change if the amount of gravity changes. The stronger the gravity, the heavier an object will be. Earth has more gravity than the moon. An astronaut who weighs 180 pounds (82 kilograms) on Earth weighs only 30 pounds (14 kg) on the moon!

ELECTRIC FORCES

All things are made of tiny particles called ***atoms***. They can have a positive or negative electric charge. An electric force happens between charged atoms. If objects have different charges, they will move closer together. If they have the same charges, they will move away from each other.

atom—the tiny particles, or pieces, of which everything is made

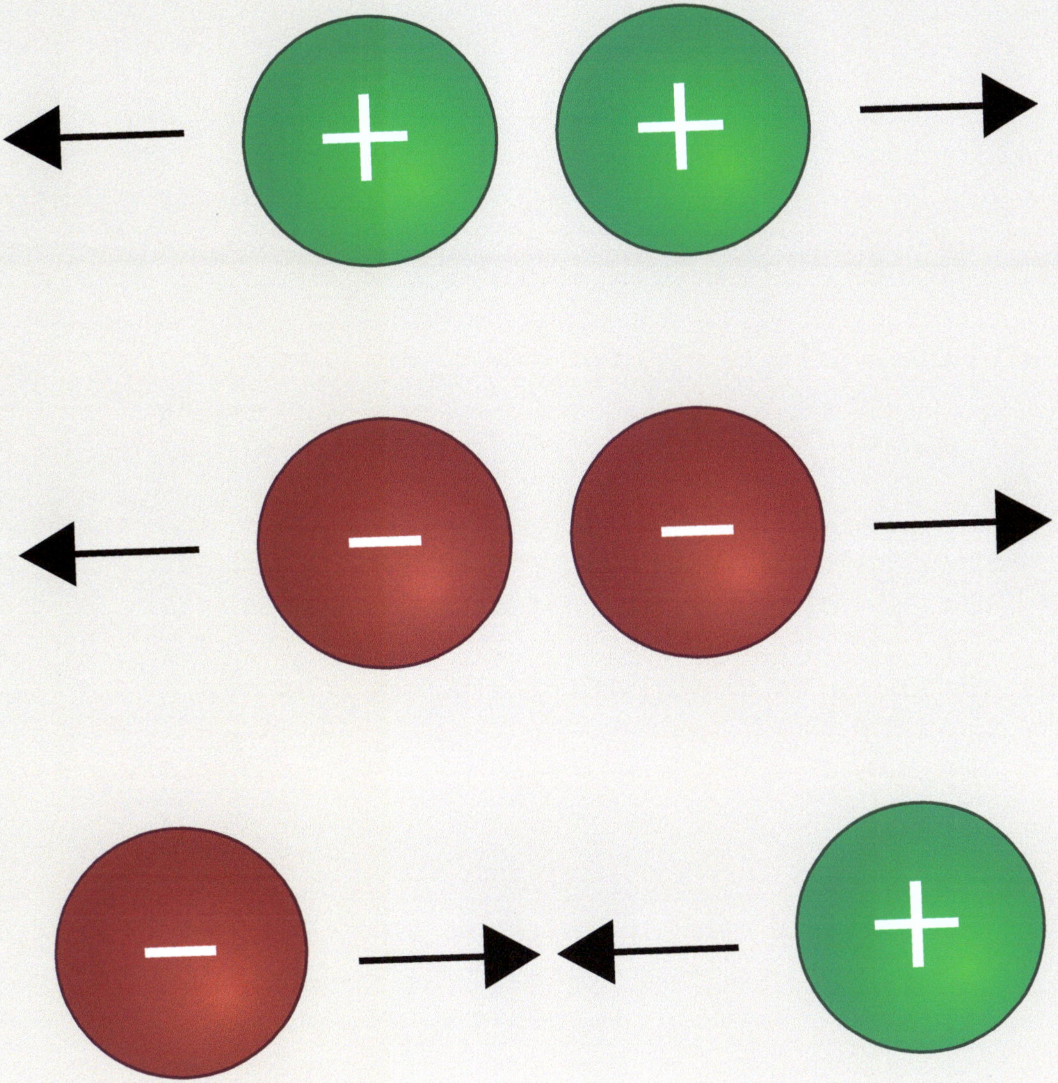

USING FORCES

We use forces all the time to move, work, and play. Often several forces act at once. A golfer hits a ball with a club. The club makes the ball go up. Gravity makes the ball come down. Friction makes the rolling ball slow down and stop.

Machines make our work easier so we use less force. Machines are made up of simple tools like wheels, ***inclined planes***, and ***pulleys***. It's hard to push a heavy box along the ground. When you put the box on a dolly with wheels, it moves much easier. An inclined plane, like a ramp, helps us move a heavy box to a higher level. Builders use cranes with pulleys to lift heavy things even higher.

inclined plane—a slanting surface that is used to move objects to different levels

pulley—a grooved wheel turned by a rope, belt, or chain that often moves heavy objects

FACT

Wheels and inclined planes do more than help get heavy objects from one spot to another. They also help people who can't walk. Wheelchairs and ramps help them go upstairs without having to climb steps.

PUSHING WITH THRUST

Thrust is a kind of pushing force. It is caused when ***exhaust*** moving in one direction pushes an object in the opposite direction. An airplane burns fuel and makes exhaust. The exhaust pushes out the back of the airplane, making the airplane move forward.

thrust—the force that pushes a vehicle forward
exhaust—the waste gases that come out of an engine

IT IS ROCKET SCIENCE!

How does a giant rocket fly all the way into space? Thrust! Huge amounts of burning rocket fuel make ***energy***. This energy produces thrust, which pushes the rocket up. A rocket must carry enough fuel to push the rocket free of Earth's gravity.

energy—the ability to do work, such as moving things or giving heat or light

FORCE EXPERIMENT

HOW FAR CAN YOU GO?

MATERIALS:

- plank of wood about 12 to 18 inches (30.5 to 45.7 centimeters) long and about 3 inches (7.6 cm) wide to use as a ramp
- long, smooth tabletop or floor
- 4 large, plastic locking blocks
- toy car with moveable wheels
- measuring tape
- dishtowel
- rubber mat

WHAT YOU DO: PART 1

1. Set up the ramp on one end of the table. Place one end of the wood plank on top of one plastic block, with the other end resting on the table (or floor).
2. Place the car on top of the ramp and let it go. Use the measuring tape to measure how far the car went before it stopped moving. Write down the answer.
3. Remove the ramp. Add one block on top of the first block, and replace the ramp. Repeat step 2.
4. Add the third block and repeat step 2 again.
5. What happens if you add a fourth block?

Did the height of the ramp affect the distance that the car went? Why?

WHAT YOU DO: PART 2

1. Set up the ramp with two blocks under it.
2. Place the dishtowel on the table with one end just under the low end of the ramp. The rest should be spread out along the table.
3. Place the car on top of the ramp and let it go. Use the measuring tape to measure how far the car went before it stopped moving.
4. Replace the dishtowel with the rubber mat. Repeat step 2 again.

On which surface did the car go farther? Did either of the surfaces let the car go farther than the two-block ramp on the smooth table? Why?

GLOSSARY

atom (AT-uhm)—the tiny particles, or pieces, of which everything is made

energy (EH-nuhr-jee)—the ability to do work, such as moving things or giving heat or light

exhaust (eg-ZAWST)—the waste gases that come out of an engine

friction (FRIK-shuhn)—a force made when two objects rub against each other; friction slows down objects

inclined plane (in-KLINDE PLANE)—a slanting surface that is used to move objects to different levels

pulley (PUL-ee)—a grooved wheel turned by a rope, belt, or chain that often moves heavy objects

resistance (ri-ZISS-tuhnss)—a force that opposes or slows the motion of an object; friction is a form of resistance

surface (SUR-fiss)—the outside or outermost area of something

thrust (THRUHST)—the force that pushes a vehicle forward

READ MORE

Braun, Eric. *Curious Pearl Kicks Off Forces and Motion: 4D, an Augmented Reading Science Experience.* Curious Pearl, Science Girl 4D. Mankato, Minn.: Capstone Press, 2018.

Hammond, Richard. *Can You Feel the Force?* New York: DK Publishing, 2015.

Spilsbury, Richard. *Investigating Forces and Motion.* Investigating Science Challenges. New York: Crabtree Publishing, 2018.

INTERNET SITES

Use FactHound find Internet sites related to this book.

1. Visit *www.facthound.com*
2. Just type in 9781977102676

www.FactHound.com®

CRITICAL THINKING QUESTIONS

1. What are the two main things forces do?
2. Name three kinds of forces.
3. Choose one simple tool we use and explain how it decreases a person's use of force.

INDEX